Mommy, Draw Stars on My Tummy

*Rhymes, Songs and Touch-Play Activities
to Stay Connected*

by Martine Groeneveld

Art by Brad Kunkle

to Wies and Sara

Grateful acknowledgment to the following for permission to quote from copyrighted material:

- Quote from *The Power of Touch* by Phyllis R. Davis. Copyright © 1999 by Phyllis R. Davis. Reprinted by permission of Hay House, Inc.
- Quote from Mr. Benjamin Scott reprinted by permission of Mr. Benjamin Scott.
- Quote from *Touching: The Human Significance of the Skin* by Ashley Montagu. Copyright © 1971, 1978 by Ashley Montagu. Reprinted by permission of HarperCollins Publishers.
- Quote from *Touch* by Tiffany Field. Copyright © 2001 Massachusetts Institute of Technology. Reprinted by permission of MIT Press.

Mommy, Draw Stars on My Tummy: Rhymes, Songs and Touch-Play Activities to Stay Connected
by Martine Groeneveld

Text copyright © Martine Groeneveld 2009
Illustrations copyright © Brad Kunkle 2009

ISBN 13: 978-0-9822959-0-8
Library of Congress Control Number: 2009904711

10 9 8 7 6 5 4 3 2 1

Printed and bound in the USA

Published by PT Book Publishing
www.ptbookpublishing.com

Book Design by Jill Ronsley, Sun Editing & Book Design, suneditwrite.com

Disclaimer

The author of this book does not dispense medical advice or prescribe the use of any technique as a form of treatment for physical or medical problems without the advice of a physician, either directly or indirectly. The intent of the author is only to offer information of general nature for families. Neither the author nor the publisher can be held responsible for any damage or injury resulting from the use of the techniques or any of the recommendations in this book. If you have any questions about the appropriateness or application of the techniques described in this book, consult a pediatric health care professional.

Contents

*Every child has a basic need to feel loved
and to connect with others.
With our heart behind our touch and voice,
we can be in loving contact with our children,
creating bonds and memories that last a lifetime.*

Foreword

The first language of love is touch; the second is dialogue. We, at the IAIM®/ World Institute for Nurturing Communication promote nurturing touch and compassionate communication for healthy family development that may last a lifetime.

We are very supportive and excited about Martine's book as part of the WINC™ global movement for the *hope* that all children will receive nurturing touch for healthy family development.

Martine's book is to encourage the continuum of family bonding through nurturing touch games for the growing child. We love her innovative touch routines and rhymes that were created to assist parents and their children to spend quality playtime together.

We are already enjoying Martine's touch routines for the growing child, and we know you will too!

—Andrea Kelly, CIMI®, CIIT™
CEO, IAIM®/dba/ WINC™
VP Board of Directors
Origin 1979, Incorporated 1986
www.winc.ws

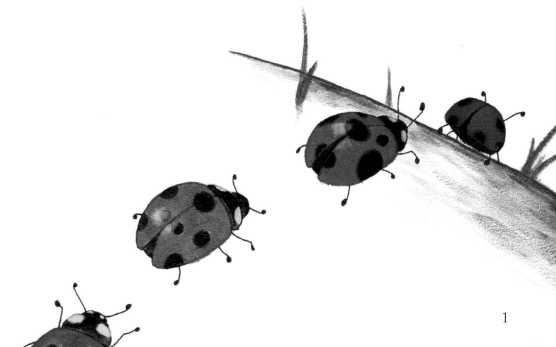

1

Introduction

Positive touch plays a major role in my family. Besides daily hugs and kisses, many activities are easily combined with loving and playful touch. We enjoy touch-play activities in the car, in line at the grocery store and before bedtime. They can be done anywhere and anytime. Parents who attend my classes engage their own children in these activities and report wonderful results.

To expand my repertoire, I searched for books on combining touch with rhymes, games and stories. I couldn't find any. Excellent books have been published about baby and child massage, but I was looking for one on touch and play. I wrote down the games and stories I knew or had created, elaborated on them and recorded their benefits. This book is the result of that effort.

Combining touch with rhyme and storytelling has been and still is a loving and fun way to connect with my children. Nurturing touch within our family has opened my heart for my children even more—I feel love and loved. When my children ask me for another rhyme or story, I see twinkles in their eyes.

This book is for you and your child to enjoy in many ways. It will show you loving and playful activities to connect with your child through touch and voice, whether you are a parent or caregiver and whether your child is your own or one who you are taking care of.

The positions and hand routines accompanying the activities are meant to be used as guidelines. You and your child can position yourselves in several ways. I don't recommend memorizing the routines; rather, following what comes naturally and what feels good to your child. Keep it simple so you and your child will be able to relax and enjoy completely.

The goal of this book is to encourage loving and positive touch in the parent-child relationship. Be creative and make the experience your own. Perhaps you can turn your child's favorite story into a touch-story. Most of all, enjoy and have fun!

Thank you for choosing this book. I wish you and your child many wonderful, precious and fun times together.

—Martine Groeneveld

A Few Notes

About lubricants:
Use a lubricant to slide easily over bare skin. Natural oils like sunflower or grape seed are light, low-odor oils that nurture the skin and won't harm your child's digestive system if accidentally ingested (for example, if oiled hands are put in the mouth). Choose an organic variety. Try it on a small area before using it on the rest of the body. Wait and observe the area for about thirty minutes to see if there is any reaction, such as redness, a rash or itching. An allergic reaction should subside after sixty to ninety minutes. If you are uncertain, don't use it.

About pressure:
The pressure of a stroke should be gentle yet firm. Light touching might be unpleasant or irritating to some children, especially newborn babies. Some of the strokes in this book are light fingertip strokes. If your child doesn't enjoy this light touch, switch to whole hand-stroking and see if your child prefers that.

About the direction of strokes:
Strokes toward the heart are considered stimulating. Strokes away from the heart are considered relaxing. If you read a story before bedtime, use strokes that lead away from the heart. If you read after nap time and would like to wake up your child, use strokes toward the heart.

About clothing:
Most of the hand routines can be done over clothing. Respect your child's desire to keep clothes on if he or she wants to do so.

About the "right moment":
Never try to do any of the activities in this book against your child's will. There might be times when your child is not in the mood and dislikes the activity. Even a small child will give cues to let you know it's not the right moment; for example, by pulling away, crying or looking away from you. Be sensitive to these cues. This will make your child feel respected.

Additional resources:
To learn more about touch and the research in this field, refer to Research and Resources at the end of this book.

Some of the information and hand movements are based on the teachings and touch routines taught by the IAIM® d/b/a World Institute for Nurturing Communication. For more information about the organization and their classes, refer to the Resources at the end of this book.

Rhymes

*Touch is a language that can communicate
more love in five seconds
than words can in five minutes.*

—Pyllis R. Davis, Ph.D.
The Power of Touch

Your child might be in any sitting position or lying on his stomach. When he's lying on his stomach, you can kneel by his head facing his feet or beside him facing his head. Use one hand or both simultaneously.

Five Little Caterpillars

Five little caterpillars crawling by my door.	*Stroke with your whole hand down the back.*
	Light stroke up.
One walked away,	*Walk with two fingers down the back.*
then there were four.	*Light stroke up.*
	Repeat these movements as you recite the rest of the rhyme.

Four little caterpillars climbing up a tree.
One walked away, then there were three.

Three little caterpillars putting on a shoe.
One walked away, then there were two.

Two little caterpillars lying in the sun.
One walked away, then there was one.

One little caterpillar crawling by my door.
One walked away, then there were … no more!

Five little caterpillars walked away,
Hoping to see you again one day.   *Wave goodbye with your hand.*

Tips

- Children like to engage. They love fill-in-the-blanks.

- For two- and three-year-olds: Keep it simple. Repeat verses and actions.
  Let your child fill in some of the words, for example: "Five little caterpillars
  crawling by my door. One … What did he do?" Stop in the middle of the line
  and let him say "walked away." Repeat with all the verses.

- For four-year-olds and older: Let them fill in the numbers.
  For example, you begin: "Four little caterpillars crawling by my door. One
  walked away, then there were … How many?"

- It's easy to change the direction of the strokes on the arms and the legs. First
  stroke up, then lightly stroke down, then walk up and lightly stroke down.
  Notice that these strokes might be more stimulating than relaxing as they
  move toward the heart.

Strokes for the ears

Massage both ears at the same time or do one side after the other.

Ants Are Playing

Ants are playing on my ear.

Over here! And over here!

Now they're hiding,

so I can't see.

Where, oh where, could

those little ones be?

Gently rub the ears between your thumb and index finger.

Massage the whole ear up and down.

Hook your fingers behind the ears

and walk them up and down.

Tips

- The ears have reflex points that correspond with the organs and other parts of the body. By massaging the ears, you can soothe or stimulate the whole body.

- Ear massage is very effective. Rubbing the ears slowly is soothing. Rubbing faster (but gently) is stimulating.

- You might like to finish by gliding your fingers from the top of the ear down to the earlobe.

- Create your own variations of this rhyme and make it into a game. For example, change the words to ants in your hair, in your neck, on your cheek, etc. You and your child might imagine all kinds of crawling creatures!

Strokes for the chest and arms

Your child might be in any sitting position or lying on her back.
Use one hand or both simultaneously.
Make small circles on the chest instead of stroking if that works better for you.

Butterfly

Butterfly, butterfly, sitting on the ground.

Butterfly, butterfly, making not a sound.

Butterfly, butterfly, spread your wings.

Butterfly, butterfly, my heart sings.

Butterfly, butterfly, fly away.

I hope to see you again one day.

1. *Rest both hands on the chest. Stroke from the midline out to the sides, down and back to the midline, making a heart shape on the chest. Repeat twice.*

2. *Stroke with your hands across the chest to the front of the shoulders and down the arms to the hands. Repeat twice.*

Repeat step 1: heart shape.

Repeat step 2: long stroke.

Tips

- Your whole hands are on the chest, parallel to each other, and your fingers point toward the head. Let your hands be light and relaxed.
- Don't put pressure on the chest. Keep your hands light.
- The chest is an intimate area. Some children don't like to be touched there, and some like it only for a couple of minutes. Respect each child's preference and move on to a different area.
- If your child is fully clothed, it is easier to make circles on the chest instead of stroking. When you move down the arm, wrap your hand around the arm and gently squeeze, skip the elbow, and continue squeezing until you reach the hand.
- You might end with a kiss on each little hand when you finish the last stroke.

Strokes for the face, arms, legs and feet

Your child might be lying on her back or sitting on your lap facing away from you.
Use one hand to do one side after the other, or both hands simultaneously.
This is a bedtime verse. Read and stroke at a slow pace to create relaxation.

Goodnight

See how the moon shines bright at night.   *Slowly circle with your*

It's time to rest, so say "night-night."   *fingertips on the head.*

(Caution: if your baby has an open fontanel, be cautious and do not massage the head)

Rest your head   *Stroke with your thumbs or fingers,*
from the middle of the forehead
to the sides and end at the
chin (heart shape).

and rest your eyes.   *Stroke with your thumbs or*
fingers over the eyebrows,
from the inside to the outside.

Kiss all your teddies sweet goodbyes.

Your cute nose,   *Stroke with a finger over the bridge*
of the nose, down to the tip.

your cheeks,	*Stroke with your thumbs or fingers over the cheeks, from the sides of the nose outward.*
your lips.	*Stroke with your thumbs or fingers over the lips, from midline to the corners.*

Doze off to Dreamland's sleepy trips.

Rest your arms. They've played so much.	*Stroke with your whole hand down the arms, from the shoulder to the hand.*
How many toys have your fingers touched?	*Make short strokes over the hands.*
Your legs were busy all day long.	*Stroke down the legs with your whole hand.*
It's time to rest, so they'll grow strong. Your sweet little tootsies	*Make short strokes along the toes, or roll them gently between your thumb and finger.*
and cute feet—	*Stroke the feet with your*
Let's tuck them snugly under the sheet.	*hands. Squeeze them gently.*
Goodnight! Goodnight! Goodnight!	*Kiss all the body parts goodnight.*

Tip

- If your child is fully clothed, fold your hands around an arm or leg and gently squeeze while you move along. Tenderly press the fingers and toes. Skip the knee and elbow joints.

13

Strokes for the back and neck

Your child might be lying on his stomach, sitting next to you or sitting on your lap facing away from you. Use one hand or both simultaneously.

Fun at the Playground

Teeter-totter up and down,

Stroke with both hands or one hand down the back. Light stroke up. Repeat two times.

Merry-go-round, all around.

Make small circles with your fingers on both sides of the spine, going down from the neck to the lower back.

Swings go high,

Open your fingers and stroke down

Swings go low,

the back, starting at the shoulders.

While slides go fast or slow.

Stroke with both hands or one hand down the back. Light stroke up. Repeat two times.

Games

*A child may thrive without hearing,
without vision or without smell.
But no child will thrive without touch.*

—Benjamin Scott, M.D. (pediatrician)

Animals, Letters, Numbers & Word Painting

With your fingers, draw an animal on your child's back or tummy. When you're finished, let him guess what it is. If he doesn't know, teach him to ask questions like, "Where does it live?" or "What sound does it make?" or "What color is it?" I guarantee that he will want you to do another one!

Tips

- While your child is trying to guess, do a few strokes over his back or tummy. When he is two or three years old, the time he takes to think will keep him focused—and lying still!
- You can play the same game with shapes, numbers and letters. Say the number or letter that follows or precedes the one you are stroking on his tummy, for example: "This is the letter that comes after D" or "This is the number that comes before 10" or "This is the letter between M and O." Based on your child's stage of development, you can make it harder or easier for him to guess.

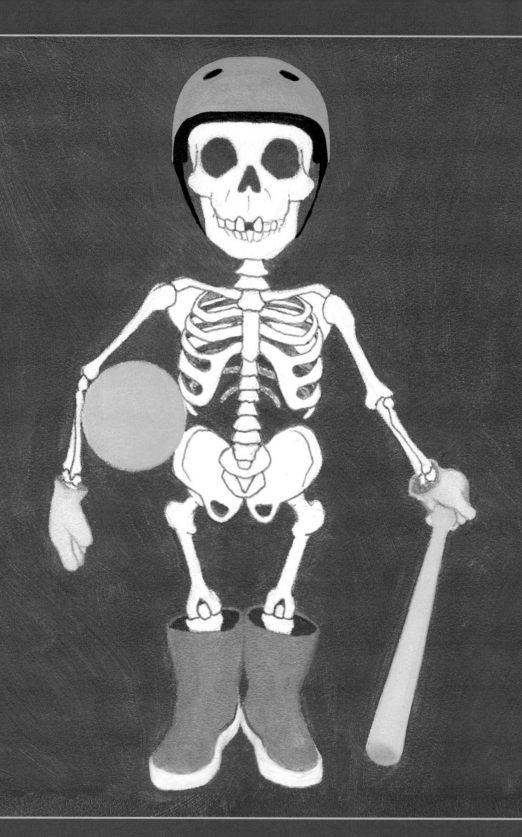

The Bone Search

Has your child discovered that her body has hard and soft parts? Does she know that the hard parts are called bones and some of the soft parts are muscles? Does she know what bones and muscles are for?

Have her search for hard and soft parts of her body. Explain to her why bones are hard (for example, "They keep your body straight") and that muscles are soft and what they are used for (for example, "They are for walking and running").

Tap on bones with your fingers to show that they are hard. Let her search for big bones (like the forehead) and tiny bones (like fingers and toes). Go to her ear and the tip of her nose and squeeze them gently to show that some special bones are soft. Move them just a tiny bit to show that these bones can move.

Tips

- Most preschoolers will be intrigued by this amazing discovery and information about their body.
- You can elaborate on this game by "drawing" organs on her tummy while explaining what these organs do.

19

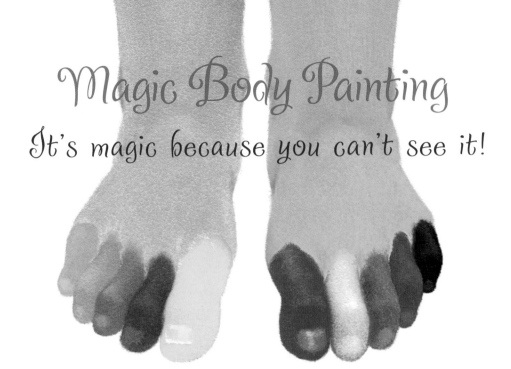

Magic Body Painting
It's magic because you can't see it!

This is an imaginative game with many variations. You can play the game on one part of the body, such as the leg, or on the whole body, making a full-body massage out of it. The game can be as quick or as long as you like, and it can be played over clothes or on bare skin.

Hold up your hand and say it is your magic paintbrush. Dip it in your magic paint (make dipping movements with your hand) and ask your child what color the paint is. Ask her what she would like to have painted in that color, such as her left leg or right arm. Stroke that leg or arm (or whatever area she chose) as if you are painting it. Make long or short strokes and circles. Alternate your hands. Be creative. Then dip your magic paintbrush in a new magic color and paint another area. Paint the whole body, making a "colorful body painting."

Tip

♥ Roll each toe or finger gently while asking your child which color it should be. She will probably end up with magic rainbow toes or fingers!

Magic Face Painting

This is the same game as the "Magic Body Painting" but played only on the face. Ask your child what he would like to be. A tiger? A prince? Maybe he'd like to have just one little spider painted on his cheek. Paint his face using your fingertips with a very light touch.

Tip

♥ Your child might enjoy playing the game on you, too!

This Piggy Went to ...

Roll each toe or finger gently as you say,
"This little piggy went to ..."

Let your child fill in the blank with his favorite places. For example, "This little piggy went to ... the zoo!" Or, "This little piggy went to a play date with ..." (*Say the name of a friend.*)

Songs

Where touching begins,
there love and humanity also begin.

—Ashley Montagu, Ph.D.
Touching

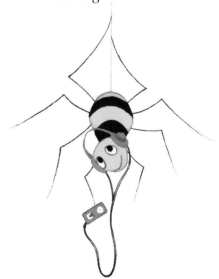

Strokes for the back, legs, arms or tummy

Your child is lying on her stomach or sitting next to you. Use one hand. This song is stimulating because of the pace and the finger movements.

Dancing Leaves

To the tune of "Jingle Bells"

Dancing leaves, dancing leaves,
dancing all around.
Oh, what fun it is to see them
twirling on the ground!

Hey!

Dancing leaves, dancing leaves,
dancing all around.
Oh what fun it is to run
in leaves upon the ground!

Let your fingers dance on the back, light and easy.
Make big and small circles, figure eights, or zig-zag down the back.

Walk with two fingers up the back to the neck.
Stroke down with your whole hand before you walk up again.

Strokes for the arms and legs

Support the wrist while holding the arm with one hand.

My Arms Are Growing Strong

To the tune of "The Farmer in the Dell"

My arms are growing strong,	*Stroke with your whole hand*
My arms are growing strong,	*from the wrist to the*
Hey-ho! Just see them grow!	*shoulder. Fingertip stroke*
My arms are growing strong.	*back to the wrist. Repeat.*
My hands are growing fast,	*Hold your child's hand in*
My hands are growing fast,	*both hands. Squeeze and*
Hey-ho! Just see them grow!	*stroke her hand, fingers and*
My hands are growing fast.	*wrist. Press all over the hand.*

Repeat the song and strokes for the legs and feet.

Tip

♡ If your child is wearing clothes with sleeves or pants, wrap your hands around the arm or leg and squeeze gently, moving up. Stroke down lightly.

Twinkles in Your Eyes

To the tune of "Twinkle, Twinkle Little Star"

Twinkles, twinkles in your eyes
Like the stars up in the skies.
Smiles so cute and eyes so bright,
Dance around and hold me tight.
Twinkles, twinkles in your eyes
Like the stars up in the skies.

My Sunshine

To the tune of "You Are My Sunshine"

You are my sunshine, my little sunshine.
You make me happy, oh can you see?
You'll always know, dear, how much I love you.
Yes, for you my love will always be.

Tips

- These two songs can accompany any nurturing stroke on the body.
- Making hearts on the body and giving kisses will go perfectly with these songs!
- Let your hands be soft and loving and do what feels natural.

27

Use one hand.

Itsy Bitsy Spider

The itsy bitsy spider climbed up the waterspout.	*Walk with two fingers up the back, leg or arm.*
Down came the rain	*Tap lightly with your fingertips as you go down.*
and washed the spider out.	*Make a long stroke from the shoulders down to the lower back (or from the shoulder to the hand, or from the thigh to the foot).*
Out came the sun and dried up all the rain.	*Make big circles on the back or little circles up the arm or leg.*
And the itsy bitsy spider climbed up the spout again.	*Walk up again with two fingers.*

Stories

A child's first emotional bonds are built from physical contact,
laying the foundation for further
emotional and intellectual development.

—Tiffany Field, Ph.D.
Touch

Dreamland

Once upon a time, late at night,
a little girl was gazing at the stars.
Big stars and little stars floated
in the dark sky.

*Make big and small circles on
your child's back.*

The moon had nestled in between
the stars and shone its
lovely white light over the dark land.

Make a moon, half or full.

Stroke its light over your child's back.

Her mommy said, "Go high in the sky.
Go left when you get to the moon
and slip behind the brightest star.
That's where you'll find Dreamland."

*Make a big, shiny star on the back.
Begin and end at the top, between the
shoulder blades.*

The girl looked up at the sky.

*Stroke down with your whole hand,
from the shoulders to the lower back.*

Just then, a star fell down.
"I can make a wish!" she thought.

Use the fingertips to stroke back up.

"I wish … I wish with all my heart
that I could float to Dreamland
with my teddy, Bart."

*End with drawing a big heart on
your child's back, followed by
a kiss!*

I wish … I wish with all my heart
that I could float to Dreamland
with my teddy, Bart.

31

Thank You, Flower

Once upon a time in a land not far away grew a beautiful flower. The sun shone from high up in the sky, warming the flower with its light. One day, the wind blew and the flower danced in the breeze. Clouds fluttered by. The sun disappeared behind one of the clouds and the sky turned gray. A tiny drop landed on the flower's leaves. Then another. And another. Drops began to sprinkle. The wind and the rain swelled, and the sky rumbled.

Draw a flower on your child's back.

Make big circles.

Let your fingers dance around on the back.

Slow down your finger movements.

With one fingertip, make tiny drops all over. Then tap lightly all over, as if drops are falling.

Thunder blew	*Drum lightly with a soft fist.*
and lightning flashed,	*Stroke back and forth with the side of your hand.*
and the flower swayed from one side to the other.	*Let your whole hand sway across the back, from side to side.*
After the last big rumble, the sky calmed down and the clouds floated away. The sun returned and shone high in the sky.	*Stroke with your whole hand down the back.*
	Make big circles.
The flower stood peaceful and proud. One leaf moved, and a tiny ladybug crawled out from under it. It had been hiding from the storm under the flower, safe and sound.	*Walk with two fingers up the back and the head. Make one long stroke down.*
Thank you, Flower!	

Tips

- Add sounds to the story for extra excitement. What is the sound of the blowing wind? What is the sound of thunder and lightning? Ask your child to make the sounds while you read the story. Most children will love this.
- After a few repetitions, your child will remember the story. Then you can turn it into a "fill-in-the-blank" game. Read the story and stop at different points to let him fill in the blank.

Afterword

This book offers you a way to stay in loving touch with your child. Nurturing touch within a family is the foundation of healthy child development. As parents, we have magic in our fingertips!

Thank you for devoting your time to reading this book. I hope it gives you many precious moments with your child. Perhaps it will inspire you to create your own rhyme or song and hand routine. If it does, I would love to hear about it, and I invite you to send me your story. Feel free to contact me at info@martinegroeneveld.com.

I wish you and your family beautiful moments, great fun and tender touches.

Research on the Benefits of Touch

Studies on the benefits of touch have been conducted widely for nearly 40 years. Since the founding in 1992 of the Touch Research Institute, a center solely devoted to the study of touch, extensive research in the field has grown tremendously.

As a registered nurse and licensed massage therapist, I have always been interested in these studies. Like many others, I believe the healing power of touch is vital to our physical and mental well-being. Scientific research confirms this belief.

Among the numerous relevant research findings, I want to share with you some that impress me the most. To learn more about the research on the benefits of touch, refer to the Resources section at the end of this chapter.

Touch stimulates weight gain in babies and improves their alertness and responsiveness.

One of the earliest studies on the benefits of touch therapy was conducted in 1986 by Dr. Tiffany Field. Dr. Field found that premature infants who received touch therapy in the form of short massages gained weight 47% faster than infants who were not massaged, even though both groups were fed the same amount of formula. The infants who received massages were more active and alert while awake, and more responsive to faces and voices. They also left the hospital six days earlier than the infants who were not massaged.

This study was later replicated by researchers in other parts of the world with similar results. Dr. Field replicated the study in 2004 with full-term babies and found faster weight gain and greater alertness among these babies as well.

These research findings are impressive in every respect. The numbers seen in the original study—47% faster weight gain and six days earlier discharge from the hospital—leave no doubt about the positive effects that touch therapy had on the infants. Furthermore, although researchers had expected the infants who received touch therapy to sleep more than the others, the massaged infants were more active, alert and responsive to faces and voices. Such alertness is crucial in intellectual development and in the process of bonding with significant others.

Touch improves cognitive performance.

In 1996, Dr. Field conducted another interesting study in which a group of preschool children received short massages twice a week for five weeks. On the very first day and throughout the duration of the study, the massaged children received better ratings on mood state, vocalization, activity and cooperation than those who received no massage. They also fell asleep more quickly at nap time.

In a 1998 study, preschoolers were divided into two groups. One group was given a set of cognitive tests before and after receiving a short massage. The other group was given the same tests, but before and after a fifteen-minute reading session in which an adult read them a story. The results revealed that the speed and accuracy of the children's cognitive performance improved after the massage. This was not the case after the story-reading session.

These studies indicate benefits of touch that we usually do not think of, such as improved mood state, vocalization, activity, cooperation, extroversion and cognitive performance.

Touch stimulates brain development.

Touch has a profound impact on how the brain develops. It stimulates the growth of dendrites, which are the connective nerve fibers between brain cells, as well as the growth of myelin sheets, the protective sheets around these fibers.

We can learn a lot about the human brain by looking at animal brains. Experiments show that animals reared as pets have heavier and thicker brains than animals reared in isolation. Also, the brains of pet animals contain up to 25% more connective nerve fibers per brain cell than the brains of isolated animals. This suggests the possibility of similar results in children.

In human beings, brain growth is complete by age seven. By that time, your child's brain has the size and weight of an adult brain. Nurturing touch received from birth into childhood may offer a child the extra benefit of enhanced brain development, and therefore optimize the brain for cognitive performance.

The thought of being able to stimulate your child's brain development through touch is remarkable.

Touch reduces aggression.

Although touch is more prevalent in some cultures than others, it is a universal need. Researchers have found that aggression and violence are less evident in cultures in which touch is customary.

In 1999, Dr. Field observed French and American preschool children on playgrounds with their parents and peers. The American children played less with their parents, talked with them less and touched them less than the French children did with their parents. Also, the American children were found to be more irritable and more aggressive toward their parents and peers.

Another study on preschool aggression, performed in 2008 by the Axelsons Institute in Sweden, found that daily touch for five to ten minutes reduced aggression in four- and five-year-old preschool children.

Cross-cultural studies have shown that Americans are some of the least tactile people in the world. Could the solution to aggression and violence be right in our own hands?

Resources

Touch Research Institute
www.miami.edu/touch-research
The Touch Research Institute is the first center in the world devoted solely to the study of touch and its application in science and medicine. The TRI team strives to better define touch with regard to how it promotes health and contributes to the treatment of disease.

Zero to Three
National Center for Infants, Toddlers and Families
www.zerotothree.org
Zero to Three informs, trains and supports professionals, policy makers and parents in their efforts to improve the lives of infants and toddlers.

Peaceful Touch
A healthy touch approach for children
www.peacefultouch.net
The Peaceful Touch program integrates healthy touch into children's activities, from games and story-telling to reading, math, and science. In Sweden more than 300,000 children practice Peaceful Touch on a regular basis.

IAIM® d/b/a World Institute for Nurturing Communication (WINC™)
www.winc.ws
The World Institute for Nurturing Communication promotes nurturing touch and compassionate communication for healthy family development through training, education and research.

Books
Sharon Heller, Ph.D., *The Vital Touch: How Intimate Contact with Your Baby Leads to Happier, Healthier Development* (New York: Owl Books, Henry Holt and Company, 1997).

Lena Jelveus, *Swedish Child Massage: A Family Guide to Nurturing Touch* (Swedish Health Institute, 2004).

Tiffany Field, *Touch* (Cambridge, Massachusetts: The MIT Press, 2003).

Tiffany Field, *Touch in Early Development* (New Jersey: Lawrence Erlbaum Associates, 1995).

Jean O'Malley Halley, *Boundaries of Touch: Parenting and Adult-Child Intimacy* (Urbana and Chicago: University of Illinois Press, 2007).

Kerstin Uvnas Moberg, *The Oxytocin Factor: Tapping the Hormone of Calm, Love, and Healing* (Cambridge, Massachusetts: Da Capo Press, 2003).

Ashley Montagu, *Touching: The Human Significance of the Skin* (New York: Harper & Row, 1986).

Frances M. Carlson, *Essential Touch: Meeting the Needs of Young Children* (Washington: National Association for the Education of Young Children, 2006).

Phyllis R. Davis, *The Power of Touch* (Carlsbad: Hay House, 1999).

Mariana Caplan, *To Touch is to Live: The Need for Genuine Affection in an Impersonal World* (Prescott, Arizona: Hohm Press, 2002).

Articles

Frances M. Carlson and Bryan G. Nelson, "Reducing Aggression With Touch," *Dimensions* (Southern Early Childhood Association) (Fall 2006): Vol. 34 # 3.

Clare La Plante, "The Kids Are All Right: Simple Massage in the Classroom Allows Children to Get in Touch with Each Other – and Themselves," *Massage Therapy Journal*, (Fall 2007).

Acknowledgments

I am forever grateful to my daughters, Wies and Sara, for being such an inspiration in my life and for giving me so much love and joy. My dear husband, Michiel, who has been behind me throughout this process, I thank you with all my heart for your support and encouragement.

Thank you to my friends, Anouk Flood, Angela Aaron and Esther de Jong, for reviewing the book and giving me valuable suggestions. I am grateful for the encouragement of Tiffany Field, a highly accomplished expert in the field of touch for children.

A special thank you to my editor and book designer, Jill Ronsley, for her guidance, expertise, patience and professionalism. I thank Margot Finke for her critiques on the rhymes.

My sister, Anja, though far away, has been a great support. Thank you for telling me you are proud of me.

Thank you Susan Campbell and Andrea Kelly, from the World Institute for Nurturing Communication, for your continued enthusiasm and enormous support.

My dear clients-turned-friends, Randy and Jennifer Roth, thank you for listening to my first concept and for your encouragement throughout this process.

I thank Duco Muller for his enormous help during the final process and Katrin Tenhaaf for her ever present support and advice.

Brad Kunkle made this book come alive with his wonderful paintings. I am forever grateful for your insights and creativity.

To all family and friends in the Netherlands and the USA, thank you for your love and support.